THE
CREATIVE MANAG...
POCKETBOOK

C000143047

John Townsend & Jacques Favier
Drawings by Phil Hailstone

"The need for creativity is more apparent than ever in today's highly competitive environment. This pocketbook provides many practical ways to help fulfil your potential."
Mervyn Simmonds, Course Director, Complete Healthcare Training

"A fascinating and eminently readable book which condenses into its 100 or so pages many interesting and immediately practicable suggestions and techniques. A 'must' for the successful manager."
Rosanne Beal, Independent Training Consultant

CONTENTS

WHAT IS CREATIVITY?

1

WHAT IS CREATIVITY?

DEFINITIONS

- The result of using the imagination rather than routine skills

- The capacity which each of us has to imagine new and useful solutions to problems

- A drive to see things other than they seem

- Lateral thinking (Edward de Bono)
  "When a low probability line of thought leads to an effective idea, there is a 'Eureka' moment and at once the low-probability approach acquires the highest probability"

PROCESS

BISOCIATION

"The bringing together of two previously
unrelated planes of thought"
Arthur Koestler
'The Act of Creation'

BISOCIATION

1 2

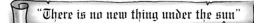

"There is no new thing under the sun" *Ecclesiastes i:8*

3

PROCESS

BISOCIATION - THE BILBOQUET

As a symbol of creativity, think of the bilboquet - the ancient French toy which has stood the test of time.

The idea is to hold the stem of the separated bilboquet with the ball hanging down on its string and, with a flick of the wrist, try to fit the ball on to the peg - thus making a complete bilboquet.

It's not as easy as it looks.
That's bisociation!

EXAMPLES
SCIENCE

Here's how bisociation worked with Pasteur's discovery of vaccination. He inoculated some chickens with a cholera virus - hoping that they would get the disease - but they survived and proved immune to all subsequent inoculations!

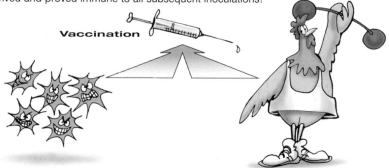

Vaccination

Cholera virus

Healthy chicken

WHAT IS CREATIVITY?

EXAMPLES

ART

Here are two bisociations we can identify in the painting of Picasso.

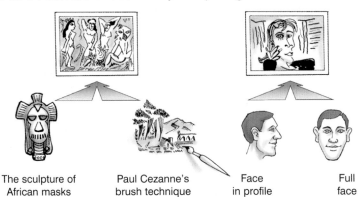

The sculpture of
African masks

Paul Cezanne's
brush technique

Face
in profile

Full
face

EXAMPLES

HUMOUR

All humour illustrates the principle of creative bisociation in that the Eureka moment is created by the listener/reader when he or she makes the connection between the two previously unrelated 'planes of thought'.

Did you know that an Irishman/ Belgian/ Newfy/Polak broke the world record for the 100 metres last week?

He ran 103 metres!

100 metres - distance   **100 metres - time**

EXAMPLES

PRODUCTS

Chipboard

Glue

Wood shavings/ sawdust

Windsurf

Sailing dinghy

Surfboard

Adhesive brush

Adhesive tape

Clothes brush

WHAT IS CREATIVITY?

IF...

- **If** Gutenberg hadn't taken part in a wine harvest, he would never have invented the printing press...

- **If** the apple hadn't fallen on Newton's head, he might never have described how the force of gravity works...

- **If** Archimedes hadn't taken a bath, he wouldn't have been the first to shout "Eureka!"...

BRAIN HEMISPHERES

Pipe dreams are fine, but an idea is only truly innovative if the right brain produces it and the left brain endorses it!

EXERCISE

Describe or draw two inventions/discoveries using bisociation

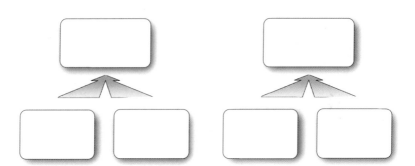

NOTES

CREATIVITY & MANAGEMENT

WHY INNOVATE?

CREATIVITY & MANAGEMENT

WHY INNOVATE?

 EXERCISE

In your opinion, what are the **five key challenges** facing your organisation over the next 10 years?

- **How to** ....

- **How to** ....

- **How to** ....

- **How to** ....

- **How to** ....

If you consider that your organisation will **not** need creativity in order to face up to these challenges, please stop reading and give this book to someone who needs it more than you.

CREATIVITY AS A MISSION

EXAMPLES

"Innovation - the generation of new ideas, new products and services and new ways of doing things - is critical to our continued vitality. Innovation flourishes when new ideas and approaches are nurtured rather than discouraged, when a positive work environment is created, when risk-taking is supported, and when experimentation is encouraged."
GTE: Vision and Values

"Technological imagination, vision and creativity must continue to provide value to our customers and future growth for our businesses."
Union Carbide: Our Mission

"To achieve our goals we must search continuously for improvement through innovation and the use of technology."
The British Airways Mission

"Our mission is to improve continually our products and services to meet our customers' needs."
Ford Motor Company: Mission and Guiding Principles

16

CREATIVITY & MANAGEMENT

AREAS FOR INNOVATION

- Product/service improvement

- Customer service improvement

- Product/service diversification

- New products/services

- More creative advertising

- Increased efficiency and quality/reduced costs

- Increased personal effectiveness and on-the-job creativity

CREATIVITY & MANAGEMENT

AREAS FOR INNOVATION
PRODUCT IMPROVEMENT

Constantly ask 'How can we improve our present products?'. Who would have predicted 20 years ago that most men would still be wet shaving in the 1990s? The success of Gillette razors over these last years has been based on constant 'bisociative' product improvement.

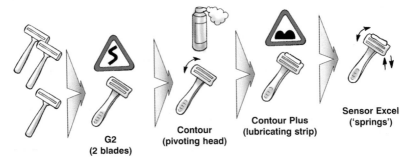

G2
(2 blades)

Contour
(pivoting head)

Contour Plus
(lubricating strip)

Sensor Excel
('springs')

AREAS FOR INNOVATION

CUSTOMER SERVICE

The creative manager is ever on the look-out for new ways of caring for the customer - especially at those 'moments of truth' when there is a direct contact with the company.

Jan Carlzon took SAS, the Scandinavian Airline, from an $8 million loss in 1981 to a $71 million profit just over a year later. One of the ways he did it was creatively paradoxical:

> "We saw that the only way SAS could use the (newly-purchased) Airbuses economically was to provide poor service to the very customers we were working to attract. How would business executives in Stockholm and elsewhere prefer to organise their travels? Would they want to fly in our roomy, new Airbuses, even if they would have few flights to choose from and required stops in Copenhagen? Or would they prefer travelling in ordinary DC-9s on frequent, non-stop flights from Stockholm, Oslo, or elsewhere directly to major cities in continental Europe? To me the answer was obvious. 'Put the Airbuses in mothballs', I said 'use the DC-9s instead'."
> **Jan Carlzon, 'Moments of Truth'**

CREATIVITY & MANAGEMENT

AREAS FOR INNOVATION
PRODUCT DIVERSIFICATION

Always be asking yourself 'What else does the customer want?'. Not content with the world-shattering success of the Walkman, Sony went on to produce some clever variations:

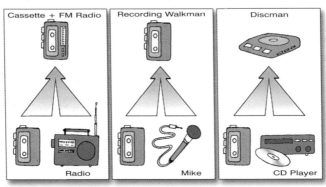

AREAS FOR INNOVATION

NEW PRODUCTS OR SERVICES

How many once-successful companies went out of business with drawers full of rejected new product or service ideas?

The 3M Company is a master of innovation. Their 'don't kill a project' philosophy allowed Spencer Silver to keep his non-sticking glue idea alive until a colleague in need of a lightly adhesive bookmark for his hymn book gave him and Art Fry the bisociation they were looking for. And the Post-It Note was born! The rest is history.

CREATIVITY & MANAGEMENT

AREAS FOR INNOVATION
CREATIVE ADVERTISING

Here are some good examples of bisociation
in advertising slogans:

SAs
loves you yeah, yeah, yeah!

(Scandinavian Airline System)

(Heathrow Airport Duty Free Shop)

Gas
the heat of the moment

(British Gas)

Our future is behind us
(Ford - new shape of Sierra boot/trunk)

(Polo - selling the nothingness!)

(Little Chef Restaurants)

AREAS FOR INNOVATION
EFFICIENCY, QUALITY, COSTS

Here are four ways in which progressive companies look for creative solutions for doing better with less:

1   **Investment Management Analysis:** Project groups of internal consultants search for ways to increase 'return on investment' (increase revenues and/or decrease costs).

2   **Total Quality Programmes:** Each employee is expected to give regular feedback to management on how to improve quality at his or her workplace.

3   **Overhead Value Analysis:** Teams of internal or external consultants conduct a survey of each staff job asking 'What does this job perform and for whom?'. Then they ask the client 'What does this job add to you and/or your performance?'.

4   **Quality Circles:** Groups of employees meet regularly to identify opportunities for improving quality throughout the organisation. Project teams implement action plans between meetings.

AREAS FOR INNOVATION

 PERSONAL EFFECTIVENESS: EXERCISE

This is a picture of busy you in your office made up of 15 shapes. Photocopy the page, cut out the shapes and rearrange them into **another** you! You'll be amazed at how many ideas you can give yourself just by doodling with the shapes.

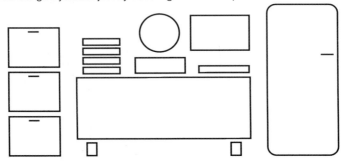

CREATIVITY & MANAGEMENT

AREAS FOR INNOVATION

 YOUR JOB: EXERCISE (Part 1)

This 'atomium' represents your job.
Write the mission or purpose of
your function in the centre and
six of your main areas of
responsibility around it.
Use only keywords.

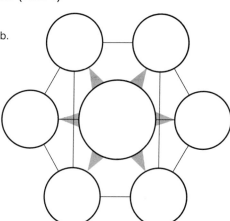

AREAS FOR INNOVATION

 YOUR JOB: EXERCISE (Part 2)

Choose one or more key areas of responsibility from your job 'atomium' where you will need creative solutions in order to adapt to the changes in your environment. What are your top three challenges?

- How to _____

- How to _____

- How to _____

The next chapter will help you to **'DIS-COVER'** your creative potential and chapter 4 will give you some ideas on how to produce ideas!

HOW CREATIVE ARE YOU?

HOW CREATIVE ARE YOU?

CREATIVITY QUIZ

On the next four pages you'll find a detailed Creativity Quiz with which to measure your creative potential to tackle those job challenges. As a warm-up exercise, take a minute to answer these three questions:

1   When did you last have a really creative idea?

This morning	Yesterday	Last week	Last month	Last year

2   What was it?

3   What motivates you to be creative?

CREATIVITY QUIZ

What is your creative potential?

Most people are much more creative than they think! This quiz will help reveal your potential and pinpoint what may be stopping you from being even more innovative.

Please read the following statements and check one of the columns opposite to indicate whether they **always**, **often**, **sometimes**, **rarely** or **never** apply to your personality, your problem-solving approach or your company/organisation. Please don't complete the **score** column until you've finished the quiz.

A. My Personality

		Always	Often	Sometimes	Rarely	Never	Score
1.	I lack confidence in myself						
2.	I value criticism						
3.	I am afraid of being different from others						
4.	My parents encouraged me to be creative						
5.	I am uncomfortable with ambiguity						
6.	I like new faces/places						
7.	I need a strong sense of order in my life						
8.	I believe that 'daydreaming' is worthwhile						
9.	I feel uneasy with people who show their feelings						
10.	I enjoy playing a role						
11.	I achieve most when I follow procedures						
12.	I rely on my feelings to guide me						
13.	I like to be known as dependable						
14.	I like to be with free-thinking people						
15.	I am reactive rather than proactive						
16.	I like looking far ahead						

TOTAL ➡ A =

B. My Problem-Solving Approach

	Always	Often	Sometimes	Rarely	Never	Score
1. When faced with a problem, I jump to conclusions						
2. When a problem arises, I am objective and analytical						
3. You need all the facts to make a decision						
4. 'Gut-feel' works for me						
5. I rely on my past knowledge of similar problems						
6. I hate working on or with details						
7. Completed staff work is the secret of success						
8. Figures and statistics give a biased picture						
9. Problems should be approached in the same way						
10. I am seen as an original problem-solver						
11. I have difficulty defining problems						
12. I use disciplined problem-solving techniques						
13. I get depressed if a problem seems too difficult						
14. When others don't take decisions, I will - if I can						
15. I like to read instructions before starting something new						
16. I believe the decision-making process is creative						
					TOTAL ➡ B =	

C. My Work Environment

	Always	Often	Sometimes	Rarely	Never	Score
1. People in my organisation think that their way is best						
2. Around here, creativity is considered as the key to survival						
3. My authority limits are strictly defined						
4. Worthwhile ideas from anywhere are accepted here						
5. Time for creative thinking is limited in this organisation						
6. Competition between employees/depts is seen as healthy						
7. I could describe my organisation as cosy and co-operative						
8. In this organisation we like to identify problems						
9. Around here, if you're creative, you're a 'dreamer'						
10. In this organisation, creative people are given 'space'						
11. Organisational procedures kill ideas						
12. I can talk freely about my ideas without them being stolen						
13. I will be stopped from suggesting new solutions						
14. Around here, good ideas can be sold regardless of results						
15. New ideas must be justified with a lot of paperwork						
16. Innovation is encouraged in this organisation						
					TOTAL ➡ C =	

Creative Potential ➡ A + B + C =

How to score

1. Please score each of your answers by writing the appropriate number of points in the SCORE column next to it. Give yourself points as follows:

- All ODD numbered questions (1,3,5,7,9 etc) should be scored:

  Never   = 5 points
  Rarely   = 4 points
  Sometimes = 3 points
  Often   = 2 points
  Always   = 1 point

- All EVEN numbered questions (2,4,6,8,10 etc) should be scored:

  Always   = 5 points
  Often   = 4 points
  Sometimes = 3 points
  Rarely   = 2 points
  Never   = 1 point

2. Once you have the scores for each answer, simply add up the total score for each of the three sections: A (My Personality), B (My Problem-Solving Approach) and C (My Work Environment).

3. Lastly, add A + B + C to find your CREATIVE POTENTIAL score.

What do my scores mean?

- Overleaf you will find a grid which shows you how to analyse your Quiz results. Please transcribe your A,B,C and Creative Potential scores to the boxes provided to make it easier to complete the analysis.

Quiz Analysis

Please write your A,B,C and Creative Potential scores in the boxes below, then read the descriptions that correspond to your scores.

Personality
A = [ ]

16-37
Your creative potential is being stifled by some of your feelings about yourself and you will be surprised how much of it will be released once you give yourself permission to be creative.

38-59
You have quite a lot of creative potential within you but parts of your personality are preventing you from expressing it. You need to work at relaxing and at asking yourself 'What have I got to lose?'. This will help remove/reduce the blockages.

60-80
Your personality predisposes you to be a highly creative person and you will be a valuable resource to others in the creative process.

Problem-Solving Approach
B = [ ]

16-37
Your problem-solving style tends to be 'by the book' and lacks creativity. Practise relaxing, forgetting some of the 'rules' and open your mind to new ideas and methods.

38-59
Your approach to problem-solving is sometimes too rigid and may result in uncreative decisions which rely too much on past solutions to similar problems. Try letting go and discover your potential for being creative!

60-80
You have an open, creative approach to problem-solving with a lot to offer to others. You should take advantage of every opportunity to create an adventurous and questioning spirit around you.

Work Environment
C = [ ]

16-37
Your working environment does not encourage creative thinking. Look at your scores for A and B. If they are on the high side, then you're sure to feel frustrated. What are you going to do about it?

38-59
It's sometimes difficult to be creative in your working environment. If you have high scores for A and B, then use some of your potential to change the environment from within. If not, maybe you fit nicely!

60-80
You work in an ideal environment for a creative person. However, if you have low A and B scores, then you should be working at developing your potential. No one is going to prevent you from contributing new ideas.

Creative Potential
A + B + C = [ ]

48-111
By now you will have realised that we all have an enormous potential to be creative - if only it is given the chance to be released. So stop your creativity being stifled by yourself or others. Just release it!

112-176
You have good creative potential very close to the surface of your conscious mind, but it is being held back by either yourself, your approach to problem-solving or your working environment. You can change any or all three - so, what are you waiting for?

177-240
You seem to be a highly creative person with lots of potential. Continue to exercise your talent by seeking new ways of using it - at home, in your hobbies and, of course, on the job.

HOW CREATIVE ARE YOU?

TOLERANCE FOR AMBIGUITY

Creative people seem to have a high tolerance for ambiguity. In other words, they readily accept that there are several ways of looking at the same thing.

For example, as you look at the cake below, you will see that there is one slice missing.

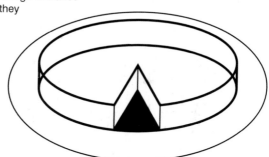

Now turn the page upside down, and you will see that slice all by itself in a dish. Is there a 'right' way of looking at the cake?

TOLERANCE FOR AMBIGUITY

If you look for a moment at the well-know 'Schröder's Staircase', you will first see it as a normal flight of steps going up from right to left. As you continue to look at it, however, it will suddenly turn upside down! Don't worry, your tolerance for ambiguity is growing!

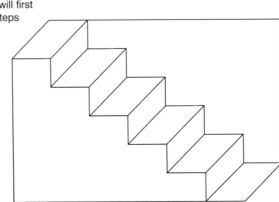

HOW CREATIVE ARE YOU?

TOLERANCE FOR AMBIGUITY

There are three ways of knowing that this is a map of France!

1. You see a map of France!
2. You see General de Gaulle (he's wearing a kepi and his eye is Paris).
3. You see former President Mitterand (his nose is Lake Geneva and his eye is Berne).

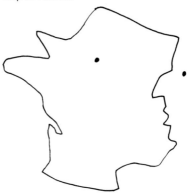

MENTAL FLEXIBILITY

 THE ALPHABETEST

This is a difficult but fun exercise. Write a story where every word begins with the subsequent letter of the alphabet - starting, of course, with A. Here's an example:

A big crocodile died, empty-fanged, gulping horribly in jerking, kicking little movements. Nonchalant old Peter Quinn ruthlessly shot the underwater vermin with Xavier yelling 'Zap!'.

Now you try! _____

_____

_____

_____

_____

_____

HOW CREATIVE ARE YOU?

MENTAL FLEXIBILITY

 WHO DOES WHAT?

As we saw earlier, creative solutions to problems need both left and right brain thinking, ie: pipe dreams and logical analysis. Here's another brain-teaser - this time a purely logical one:

Jane Simpson, Ted Anderson, Fred Harris, Sam Carter and **Peter Thomas** work for a small company and their jobs are **Clerk, Secretary, Manager, Accountant** and **Lawyer** - but not in that order! Here are some clues as to who does which job. You have seven minutes to put a name to each job.

- *The secretary bandaged the lawyer's finger when he cut it using the former's nail file*

- *While the manager and lawyer were away on a business trip, the accountant deducted half a day's pay from Thomas and Carter for taking the afternoon off to go to a football match*

- *The accountant is an excellent bridge player and Anderson admires his ability*

- *Thomas invited the secretary to lunch but his invitation was not accepted*

The answers are upside down at the bottom of page 108

HOW CREATIVE ARE YOU?

MENTAL FLEXIBILITY

 PUZZLES

Now for two puzzles for which you'll need a lot of right brain bisociative creativity to solve!

The idea is to make each of the following equations 'balance' (ie: the left side must really equal the right side) by adding no more than **one straight line** to each. In neither case may the straight line be through the equals sign to cancel it out!

- **5 + 5 + 5 = 550**

- **VI = I**

The answers are upside down at the bottom of page 108.

CREATIVITY BLOCKERS

The Creativity Quiz probably brought to light some of the things which are blocking your creative potential. Here are some other creativity blockers to be aware, and beware, of:

- Habit
- Fear of making mistakes
- Upbringing
- Language
- Fear of consequences
- The weight of previous 'models'
- Absolute truths
- Principles
- Fear of change
- Comfort with patterns

- Certainty
- Beliefs
- Self-doubt
- Rational thought
- Fear of appearing childish
- Specialisation
- Unwillingness to 'play games'
- Age
- Lack of time
- Politeness

"The brain is a wonderful thing - it switches on as soon as you wake up in the morning and doesn't switch off again until you arrive at the office". *Irish proverb*

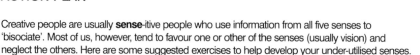

HOW CREATIVE ARE YOU?

PREPARING FOR CREATIVITY

ACTION PLAN

Creative people are usually **sense**-itive people who use information from all five senses to 'bisociate'. Most of us, however, tend to favour one or other of the senses (usually vision) and neglect the others. Here are some suggested exercises to help develop your under-utilised senses.

LOOK
- Next time you're in a garden or park, pick out 15 kinds of green
- Try writing a description of one of your favourite beauty spots

LISTEN
- Listen to a well-known piece of music and pick out every instrument - then try it with an unknown piece
- From time to time stop and distinguish 10 separate sounds from the 'cacophony' around you

TOUCH
- Every so often, close your eyes; reach out like a blind person and touch objects around you - how will you remember what they feel like?

TASTE
- Can you distinguish a Bordeaux wine from a Beaujolais - blindfolded?
- Give yourself some other 'taste tests' and try to describe the tastes to someone else
- Let tastes take you back in time!

SMELL
- Regularly conjure up pleasant smells in your mind (perfume, wood smoke, sea air) and see/feel/hear where they transport you!

PREPARING FOR CREATIVITY

 CROSS-SENSING EXERCISE

Now try and be creative with your senses! Poets are able to create experiences in their readers' minds by using descriptions that use several senses at the same time.
Examples:

- The hard, dark, empty sound of thunder
- The pungent, gold and amber smell of crackled burning leaves
- "I heard cathedral bells dripping down the alleyways" *(Paul Simon)*
- One we all remember: "They call me mellow yellow" *(Donovan Leitch)*

Try some cross-sensing descriptions yourself:

_____

_____

_____

_____

" I believe that humanity should accept, as an axiom for its conduct, the principle for which I have laid down my life - the right to investigate. It is the credo of free men - this opportunity to try, this privilege to err, this courage to experiment anew. We scientists of the human spirit shall experiment, experiment, experiment."

Roger Bacon (c 1220-1292)

"There is a desperate need for the creative behaviour of creative individuals. With scientific discovery and invention proceeding geometrically, passive and culture-bound people cannot cope with the issues. Unless individuals, groups and nations can imaginatively construct new ways of relating to these changes, the lights will go out. We must make new and original adaptations as rapidly as science introduces change, or annihilation will be the price we pay for our lack of creativity."

Carl Rogers (Quoted in Brain/Mind Bulletin, September 1990)

PRODUCING
CREATIVE IDEAS

PRODUCING CREATIVE IDEAS

TECHNIQUES, TOOLS & TRIGGERS

This chapter is divided into three sections:

1. Techniques

Here, we describe 10 'ready-to-use' problem-solving techniques in terms of:

 Objectives/ description/applications

 Instructions

 Materials needed

On the reverse side of each description is a practical example of how the technique has been used in one of our creativity sessions.

2. Tools

In this section, you'll find three useful tools for use in any creative problem-solving situation:

- Mind mapping
- The 5-point scoring system
- Visualisation

3. Triggers

Several of the creativity techniques rely on or can be supplemented by outside 'triggers'. This section consists of simple but evocative drawings of animals and objects to be flipped through and selected at random. The techniques for which the trigger cards can be used are marked with this logo:

PRODUCING CREATIVE IDEAS

BRAINSTORMING

 To surface as many ideas as possible on any 'how to ....?' problem using the classic method of round-the-table suggestions.

- Select a group leader/scribe and describe the problem. Using a flipchart, ask each member in turn to suggest a solution.

- Record **all** ideas on the flipchart (however way-out or seemingly silly) and, if possible, number them to ease final selection.

- Encourage and provoke team members to give ideas or pass. After two members have 'passed' switch to 'popcorn' mode where anyone can call out an idea as it comes. No evaluation of ideas should be permitted. Crazy and 'stupid' ideas should be encouraged as well as those which 'piggyback' on others.

- Once the leader feels there are enough ideas, move to the evaluation phase to choose one or more viable solutions using a consensus selection method, eg: the 5-point scoring system (see page 71).

- ✓ Round or U-shape table
- ✓ Flipchart and markers
- ✓ Notebook per participant
- ✓ Trigger cards could help surface more unusual ideas

PRODUCING CREATIVE IDEAS

BRAINSTORMING

EXAMPLE

Here's an example taken from one of our creativity seminars:

Problem: An umbrella manufacturer has an unsold stock of 500,000 old-fashioned, black umbrellas in the warehouse. How to liberate the warehouse space while minimising costs?

Ideas: • Publicity carriers for firms • Give out free in rainy town centres • Use material to make hats and coats • Use upside down as irrigation devices • Sell to UK • Sell two as 'CarryKit' to Third World • Burn down warehouse and collect insurance • Make giant sculpture • Use struts as bicycle spokes • Send to northern Norway as snow-bound airport signalling device (several hundred could be opened and closed to spell out messages to approaching aircraft!) • Sell to Africa as parasols, etc

Best three after 5-point vote:
- Use upside down as irrigation devices
- Sell two umbrellas + a pole as a 'CarryKit' to Third World
- Make a giant sculpture of an umbrella as publicity

PRODUCING CREATIVE IDEAS

NYAKA (DEFECT ANALYSIS)

 To build on a group's natural critical abilities in order to improve a product, service or situation by listing and then finding remedies for its key defects (from the French 'il n'y a qu'a ...': All you have to do is ...)

- Select a group leader/scribe and describe the problem. Draw a vertical line down the centre of a flipchart sheet.

- Set a time limit (20 mins?) for the group to list as many 'things which are wrong with' the product, service or situation as possible. Mark each idea in the *left* column.

- Ask the group to brainstorm (in turn or 'popcorn') *a remedy for each of the defects listed* with a view to proposing an improved product, service or action plan which eliminates as many of the defects as possible. Mark each remedy against the relevant defect in the right column.

- Get the group to agree on a new or improved product, service or action plan. Consensus is usually easy to obtain but, if not, the leader should propose an idea selection method such as the 5-point scoring system (see page 71).

✔ Round or U-shape table

✔ Flipchart and markers

✔ Notebook per participant

✔ Trigger cards could help surface more unusual remedies

PRODUCING CREATIVE IDEAS

NYAKA (DEFECT ANALYSIS)
EXAMPLE

Problem: How can we improve the efficiency of the manual paper hole-punch (for binders)?

WHAT'S WRONG (DEFECTS)	REMEDY? (NYAKA)
1. Can't make holes in many pages at a time	Make opening adjustable to number of pages to punch
2. Often leaves oily marks on paper	Make with materials which don't need lubrication
3. You can only use it for punching holes	Add more uses/functions
4. Needs a lot of physical effort for results obtained	Adapt the spring/operating system to facilitate use
5. Takes up too much space on the desk	Gain space by combining with another device
6. You can never find it when you need it	Attach it to the binder

Solution: Make binders with a ring mechanism which doubles as a simple hole-punch.

PRODUCING CREATIVE IDEAS

merlin

 To improve a product, service or situation by subjecting it to a number of hypothetical changes in terms of size, use, functioning, etc. The Merlin technique can be used working alone or with a group.

- Using two flipcharts or A4 sheets, label four columns: **Enlarge, Reduce, Eliminate** and **Reverse**.

- Brainstorm, for 10 minutes on each, (crazy) ways to:
  Enlarge the product, service or situation, eg: quadruple the price; instead of serving one market segment we expand the service to the whole world/galaxy/universe; what if the unsatisfactory situation concerned *every single customer*?
  Reduce everything about the product, service or situation.
  Eliminate the problem entirely. What would happen if it didn't exist? How to replace it?
  Reverse the way in which the product, service or situation functions, ie: instead of us serving the customer, what if the customer served us?!

- Review four lists for feasible ideas. Trigger concrete suggestions from crazy ideas. Elaborate. Shortlist. Select best idea.

If conducted with a group:

✓ Round or U-shape table

✓ Two flipcharts and markers

✓ Notebook per participant

(49)

PRODUCING CREATIVE IDEAS

mERLIN

EXAMPLE

This example comes from one of our creativity workshops. The problem was to find four viable ideas to improve the appearance, utility and/or marketability of the pocket comb. Here are some selected ideas from the four lists and the 'winners'.

Enlarge	Reduce	Eliminate	Reverse
• Comb for lawns • Space comb for satellite debris • Bicycle 'rack' • CD 'rack' • Crop spray comb • Roofing material • Comb for fishing (instead of net)	• Moustache comb • Finger combs for wavy hair • 'Pen' comb • Chromosome comb • Eyebrow comb • Doll's comb • Folding comb	• Bald cream (for shiny heads!) • Disposable combs (tear-off strip of card comb in bathroom dispenser) • Make scissors • 'Bald is beautiful' campaign on TV	• Blow-wave drier • Fixed comb on wall (you move your head!) • Public combing machine (like photo booth with computerised comb movements for different hair styles)

PRODUCING CREATIVE IDEAS

FEATURES MATRIX

 To use a matrix device in order to provoke forced and unorthodox bisociations between two characteristics of a product, service or situation.

- Having selected the problem (examples: • How to expand product line or services offered? • How to reduce customer complaints?) identify the two axes for the Features Matrix, ie: two characteristics which can be compared, such as: • Products or services/Their applications • Products or services/Customer types • Types of complaint/Months of the Year.

- Plot all the presently known combinations between the two sets of characteristics (mark with **X**).

- Encourage unorthodox combinations and plot ideas (mark with ▲).

- Elaborate on new ideas for combinations on a separate sheet (if the problem is an unsatisfactory situation the ▲ will indicate when the situation does *not* occur so you now analyse reasons why not).

- Select best/most likely.

If conducted with a group:

☑ Round or U-shape table

☑ Flipchart and markers

☑ Notebook per participant

APPLICATIONS				
PRODUCTS	1	2	3	4
Product 1	X	X		
Product 2	▲	X	▲	
Product 3	X	X	X	▲
Product 4		▲		X

51

FEATURES MATRIX

EXAMPLE

Problem: A manufacturer of homecare products wishes to identify new markets and/or new products.

Features Matrix Axes:

1. Product categories (bath/shower; clothes care; furniture/floor care; air care; laundry; etc)
2. Customer categories (children, teens, newly weds, singles, couples, middle aged, retired)

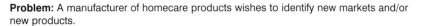

P	CUSTOMER			
R		1	2	3	4
O	Product 1	X	X		
D	Product 2	▲	X	▲	
U	Product 3	X	X	X	▲
C	Product 4		▲		X

'Forced' but Viable Associations:

- Special kid's range of bath/shower products
- 'First Home' care kit for newly weds and students (includes whole product range)
- Teens clothes fashion enhancers (jeans shrinker, glitter spray, temporary colours, etc)
- Laundry rinse for children (with mild disinfectant for cuts and scratches and/or insect repellent and fruit fragrances)

PRODUCING CREATIVE IDEAS

EUREKA!

To solve a problem in an illogical way by making forced associations with totally unrelated words/themes. Eureka works best in a group problem-solving situation.

- Select a leader/scribe. Before describing the problem to the group, choose at random three trigger cards from the end of this chapter and draw a column for each on a flipchart sheet. Show the trigger cards to the group or photocopy them and stick one at the top of each column.

- Ask the group members to call out (in turn) the first word that comes to their minds when they think of the item on the trigger card. Fill each column with these 'free associations'.

- Now describe the problem to be solved and ask team members to propose solutions which *use at least one word from each of the three columns*. Write solutions (most will be totally ridiculous) on a separate sheet.

- Review the list of solutions and brainstorm concrete suggestions by triggering from crazy to feasible ideas.

- Select best idea and elaborate.

- ✓ Round or U-shape table
- ✓ Two flipcharts and markers
- ✓ Notebook per participant
- ✓ Three trigger cards from this chapter (photocopy and stick)

PRODUCING CREATIVE IDEAS

EUREKA!

EXAMPLE

Problem: How to improve communications between subsidiaries in a multinational company?

Trigger cards chosen and examples of free associations made:

SPIDER	GUITAR	ELEPHANT
• Web	• Music	• Giant
• Network	• Tapes and records	• Tusk
• Flies	• Spain	• Disappearing species
• Fear	• 6 Strings	• Ivory
• Creepy	• Tuning	• Memory
• Useful	• Creative	• Heavy
• Cannibal	• Knopfler	• Africa

Ideas: ➤ Network + Tuning + Memory = Introduce a computerised and updated communications map to keep subsidiaries in tune and improve the corporate memory. ➤ Web + Tapes + Disappearing Species = Record and distribute a regular information video to all subsidiaries to avoid them feeling 'doomed to extinction'. ➤ Fear + Creative + Africa = Award a 'not-invented-here' annual prize to the subsidiary which can prove it has used the most ideas from other subsidiaries, ie: is not afraid of creative ideas coming from Africa - or anywhere!

PRODUCING CREATIVE IDEAS

BRAINFAXING

To find a creative solution to a negative scenario which you want to avoid by building on the ideas of 4-6 other participants who are at different locations within the organisation - but linked by a fax machine.

- Inform 4-6 participants of the rules for Brainfaxing. Fax each of them a short description of a **negative future scenario** which you'd like to avoid with some creative solutions (Fax 1).

- First ask all participants to write one possible reason why this scenario could happen (directly onto the fax under your description - max 2 lines) and fax the sheet (Fax 2) to the next participant in an agreed sequence (participant A faxes his/her idea to participant B, B to C, etc).

- Participants then think about the reason they have received, suggest one way of avoiding it (writing directly onto the original) and fax the whole thing back to you (Fax 3).

- Review each suggestion (alone or with the group) and select the most feasible.

- One fax machine per Brainfaxer location

- Trigger cards could help surface more unusual ideas

55

PRODUCING CREATIVE IDEAS

BRAINFAXING

EXAMPLE

Negative scenario (Fax 1): It is January 1st 2005. Our organisation no longer exists. The reason for its disappearance is:

Examples of possible reasons (Fax 2)	Examples of suggestions (Fax 3)
Our managers were incompetent	Hire new, and train existing, managers
Our president ran off to the Cayman Islands with his secretary and all the cash	Reinforce/introduce new control systems
A consumer group successfully campaigned against our products	Set up an active PR department NOW!
We were taken over by a small Hungarian competitor	Buy out the Hungarian company before it's too late!
We were in the contaminated zone when the nuclear power station exploded	Move the HQ and factory to a 'safe' zone
A competitor brought out a product that made ours obsolete	Increase the R&D budget; diversify into other product areas

Solution: Set up a joint venture with the Hungarian company • Reinforce management controls • Increase R&D budget by 25% • Diversify into XYZ

PRODUCING CREATIVE IDEAS

ANALOGIES

To look at a problem in a new way by asking a group to compare it to a completely different situation (analogy) thus triggering creative ideas. Often, the original analogy has disappeared by the time you make your final selection.

- Describe the problem to be solved and ask the group to brainstorm a list of analogies. The best way to come up with an analogy is to think of the problem and say 'It's a bit like...'. Alternatively, the group leader could 'impose' an analogy from which to work. For example, a fairy tale (Snow White, etc) or a situation from history (the Battle of Waterloo, etc).

- Select an appropriate analogy from the list (if necessary, use the 5-point scoring system).

- Ask the group to compare the problem at hand to the analogy and come up with suggested actions. For example, in the Snow White analogy, the seven dwarves could be smaller companies or departments who could help you solve your 'wicked witch' problem.

- Note ideas as they come and encourage triggers to new, unrelated solutions.

- Select solution(s) and elaborate.

PRODUCING CREATIVE IDEAS

ANALOGIES

EXAMPLE

Problems: How to develop the employment agency business in the face of stiff competition?

Analogies: 'It's a bit like...' A trapper venturing into the Canadian tundra surrounded by bears and Indians • Building a hotel in the middle of the Sahara desert • Selling fans to the Patagonians.

Selected: Hotel in the desert.

Triggers: From 'deserts' to new markets to be explored - despite the 'heat'. From 'new markets' to the example of banks creating specific products and services for the under 18's so as to keep them as adult customers. From the idea of the under 18's to the Eureka suggestion of offering computer seminars, factory visits and talks from occupational psychologists to 12-15 year olds. This real case (in Switzerland) provided the organisation not only with future clients but also some interesting free PR in the national press.

IDENTIFICATION

To find innovative solutions to any problem by asking team members to literally 'identify' themselves with the problem. A sensitive but powerful technique with a lot of 'heart' involved!

- Select a leader/scribe, stand at a flipchart and describe the problem to be solved.

- Ask each team member, in turn, to *identify* with the problem (product or service to be improved/created; unsatisfactory situation/conflict to be resolved, etc) for 30-60 seconds. In doing so, the individual must imagine s/he is *inside* the problem and describe what it feels like, what is seen, what is happening, etc, using as much imagination as possible. Identification works best when speakers close their eyes and turn away from the group.

- As each team member speaks, note down key items (nouns, adjectives, feelings, etc) on the flipchart. Use speaker's actual words. Others note solution ideas as and when they come.

- Review list and brainstorm how the words and feelings described could trigger solutions to the problem.

- Select best and elaborate.

- ✓ Round or U-shape table
- ✓ Flipchart and markers
- ✓ Notebook per participant

IDENTIFICATION

EXAMPLE

This example is quoted by the Synectics Consulting Group from Boston.

Problem: A manufacturer of clay pigeons was seeing sales declining as a result of complaints from residents near shooting ranges that pieces of clay pigeons were falling onto lawns and damaging mowers.

Identification: Each member of the small staff was asked to 'identify' with a clay pigeon! One team member intoned "I am flying through the air, happy as can be when ... ouch! I've been hit in the wing. I'm falling, falling ... crash! I've landed on somebody's lawn. Oh, I'm so ashamed, I wish I could melt into the ground!"
"Eureka", shouted another team member, "we must make our pigeons out of ice!"
"And add fertiliser to the water before we freeze it?", asked another, helpfully.

PRODUCING CREATIVE IDEAS

WRONG RULES

 To improve the effectiveness/quality or reduce the costs of an operation by applying the 'wrong rules' to the situation. This technique can be used working alone or with a group.

- Select one of the sets of rules overleaf (or find another set) which is 'closest' to the operation whose effectiveness you wish to improve. Use a flipchart pad for ideas as they come.

- Go through each Golden Rule in turn and try, by all means possible, to apply it to your problem. Encourage wild ideas. If you can't seem to apply one of the Golden Rules, move on to the next. The purpose of the exercise is not to force a 'mirror' of the rules but to surface creative ideas, however they come.

- Review the list of ideas. Select those which are most feasible and elaborate an action plan.

If used with a group:

✓ Round or U-shape table

✓ Flipchart and markers

✓ Notebook per participant

(61)

PRODUCING CREATIVE IDEAS

WRONG RULES

THE MACTAVISH RULES

Legend has it that during the Crimean War, the gun crews of the horse-drawn Russian artillery were little more than cart drivers, leaving the loading, aiming and firing of their cannon to the master gunner - until they learned the six golden rules of Hamish McTavish and increased their fire power and strike record tenfold!

1. Gun crews will halt their carriages with the cannon **facing** the enemy
2. Each gun crew will be responsible for the loading of the cannon
3. One gunner from each crew will light the cannon
4. Another gunner will aim the cannon and observe the trajectory of the shot
5. If the target is missed, the same gunner will re-aim the cannon
6. This procedure will be repeated as often as is necessary

Applications
- Strategic planning meetings
- Who should do what?
- How to reduce costs/increase quality/use headcount more

PRODUCING CREATIVE IDEAS

WRONG RULES

RULES FOR FLOURISHING FLORISTS

1. Keep all flowers in water at all times
2. Regularly cut the ends of the flowers' stems
3. Keep flowers at a satisfactory and constant temperature
4. Arrange and stock flowers loosely, not in tightly-packed vases
5. Always remove withered flowers from bouquets
6. Add cut-flower fertiliser to water regularly

FIRE EVACUATION PROCEDURE

1. Walk in an orderly manner towards evacuation points
2. Avoid unnecessary conversation to permit communication with the fire services
3. Immediately clear emergency exits
4. Regroup in the parking areas
5. Await instructions
6. Do not re-enter the building until instructed by the fire services

PRODUCING CREATIVE IDEAS

WRONG RULES

EXAMPLE

Problem: How to be more effective as a secretary? Using the '**Rules for Flourishing Florists**' as a trigger, set six 'improvement' objectives:

1	*Keep all flowers in water at all times.*	Organise a regular 'coffee meeting' with my boss to discuss mutual needs/problems, etc.
2	*Regularly cut the ends of the flowers' stems.*	Avoid piles of paperwork with a programme of regular filing.
3	*Keep flowers at a satisfactory and constant temperature.*	Agree with my boss on a precise, written job description.
4	*Arrange and stock flowers loosely, not in tightly-packed vases.*	Not to accept regular menial and time-consuming tasks from my boss. Agree on type and frequency of such tasks.
5	*Always remove withered flowers from bouquets.*	Ensure that my in-tray is cleared by 1600 hrs. each day to allow for 'planning' tasks.
6	*Add cut flower fertiliser to water regularly.*	Draw up a personal development plan and agree necessary training with boss.

PRODUCING CREATIVE IDEAS

FRAME UP/DOWN

 A technique developed by Mark Brown to help problem-solvers move out of their frame of reference regarding a problem and see it from another angle - and trigger solutions.

- Describe the problem to be solved and select a word or phrase to symbolise it. A real example from an airline session was: 'How to get more pilots to want to fly F-27s instead of DC-9s?'

- Using the mind mapping technique (see page 67) start to frame up and down as ideas come. A frame up is a concept that is larger than and yet includes the lower frame along with many others. In the example, a frame up from F-27 would be 'airplane' and then up again to 'airline' or 'flying club'. A frame down is an aspect or example of the higher frame. From F-27, you might frame down to 'cockpit', 'passengers' or 'a pink F-27', and from 'cockpit' down to 'heating system'. Circle or 'cloud' your frames as the mind map progresses. Example overleaf.

- Note ideas/solutions as they come then move on to more frames. For example, the phrase 'flying club' above gave us the idea of allowing airline pilots to buy shares in the F-27s with their flying hours so that they could own part of a plane when it was 'retired' from the airline.

- Review all solutions noted for feasibility, elaborate on best and implement.

If used with a group:

- ✓ Round or U-shape table
- ✓ Large white-board with markers
- ✓ Notebook per participant
- ✓ Trigger cards could help

65

PRODUCING CREATIVE IDEAS

EXAMPLE

Here is an abbreviated example from Mark Brown's 'Dinosaur Strain' (Element Books). The company makes wall-coverings and the starting point is 'How to increase the sales of paint?'.

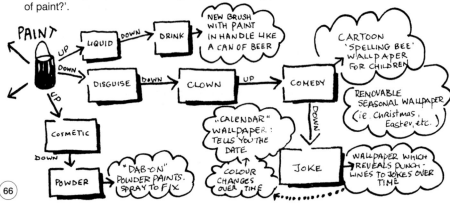

66

PRODUCING CREATIVE IDEAS

TOOLS

MIND MAPPING

Mind mapping is a brainstorming tool which allows you to surface and build on ideas rapidly and creatively. Developed by Tony Buzan, Peter Russell and Mark Brown in the mid-1970s, mind mapping is now being used by creative managers all over the world as a note-taking and note-making device.

The principle behind mind mapping is that the process of creativity is organic rather than linear and that creative thoughts grow like the branches of a tree rather than in lines like in a book or on a computer screen. When applied to problem-solving, the guidelines are as follows:

- Start in the middle of the page with the problem (keyword or phrase)
- Put main ideas as keywords on 'trunks' radiating out from the middle
- Note sub-ideas as keywords on 'branches' of trunks and then 'twigs'
- Wherever possible use colour plus logos or pictures instead of words
- Line 'triggered' or related ideas with dotted lines 'Blob' finished
  sections - **but this is a linear description, so - PTO!**

TOOLS

MIND MAPPING: PRINCIPLES

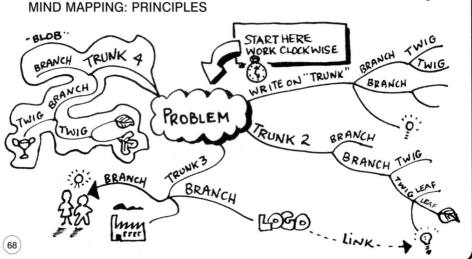

PRODUCING CREATIVE IDEAS

TOOLS

MIND MAPPING: EXAMPLE

Problem: What could a writer include in a pocketbook for creative managers?!

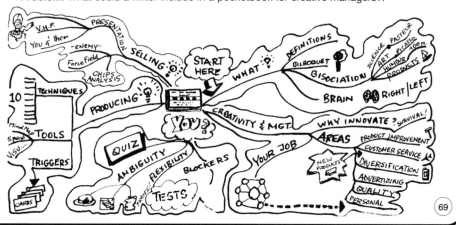

69

PRODUCING CREATIVE IDEAS

TOOLS
 MIND MAPPING: EXERCISE

Now it's your turn. Use this page to quickly brainstorm with yourself ways in which European governments can deal with the very real problem of state pensions in the years 2005 to 2020 - too many 'baby boom' pensioners and not enough money!

PENSIONS 2005

PRODUCING CREATIVE IDEAS

TOOLS

THE 5-POINT SCORING SYSTEM

Whichever creative problem-solving technique you use, the moment will always come when you have to select the 'best' idea. If you've been working in a group, this is always difficult and delicate because it's natural for everyone to think **their** idea is the best.

One way to get over this problem democratically is to allow every participant 5 points which they can award in any way they wish to any one of five of the suggested solutions (except their own!).

In other words, they can give all 5 points to one suggestion, give 4 to one suggestion and 1 to another, give 2 points to one, 2 to another and 1 to another, or 2+1+1+1, etc.

The solution which gets the most points is automatically selected. In the case of a tie, a simple vote will usually do the trick.

PRODUCING CREATIVE IDEAS

TOOLS

VISUALISATION

Visualisation is a simple tool which is often neglected in the creativity process because of lack of time or fear of the 'touchy-feely' aspect of closing one's eyes in public!

Highly creative people will tell you that once they have an idea, they take some time to make a clear and detailed picture of the final, implemented solution. Some song writers, for example, create the album cover in their mind before composing the first song. Soccer players and skiers see themselves creating new moves over and over in their minds. Painters visualise the finished canvas.

Whenever **you** have an idea, stop and savour it. Elaborate on it mentally. See it working in practice. Play that film over and over. When intention starts to take on a concrete form, the steps in between don't seem so daunting. Soon all you have to do is ..... go for it!

PRODUCING CREATIVE IDEAS

TRIGGERS

TRIGGER CARDS

On the next pages are a series of trigger cards - drawings of animals and objects which will help trigger 'bisociative' ideas during the creative problem-solving process. The principle is simple:

- You, or the group leader, flip through the pages and select a picture at random. (Once you think you have exhausted the possibilities from these pictures, use any children's book or even a dictionary.)

- Concentrate on the picture and try to imagine how that animal or object could possibly have any connection with the problem you are trying to solve. The crazier the idea the better - it may trigger another, more feasible solution.

The creative problem-solving techniques for which these trigger cards are most useful have been marked with this logo:

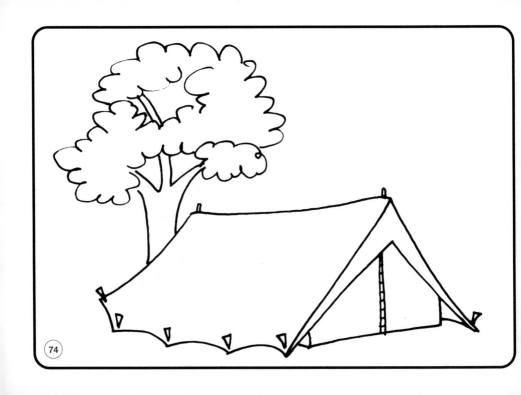

(74)

75

76

77

78

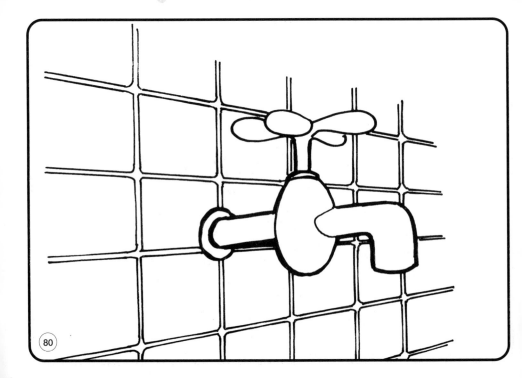

80

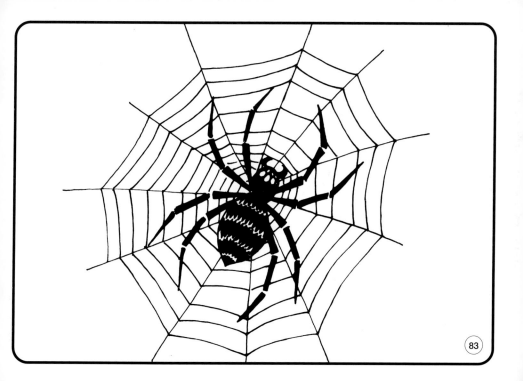

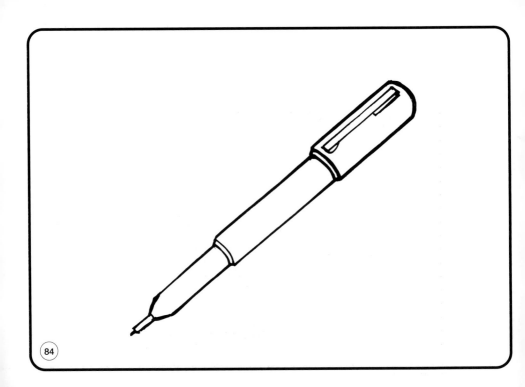

84

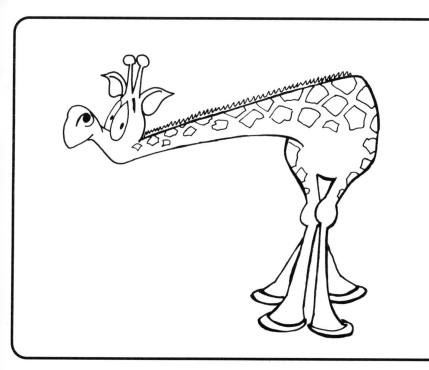

85

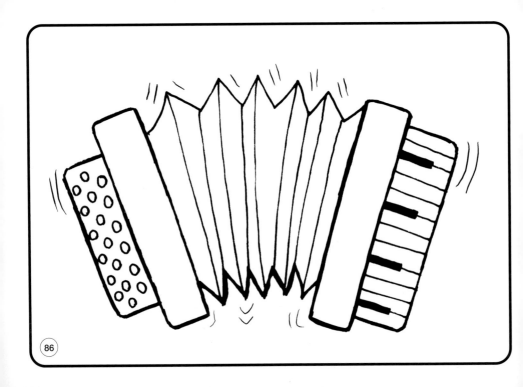

86

87

89

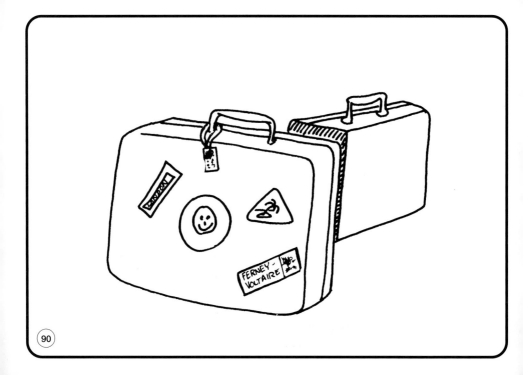

91

93

94

95

96

SELLING CREATIVE IDEAS

SELLING CREATIVE IDEAS

CREATIVITY & MANAGEMENT

'IT'S NOT CREATIVE UNLESS IT SELLS'
David Ogilvy (advertising guru)

SELLING CREATIVE IDEAS

THE ENEMY

"I have seen the enemy and he is us."

It's true that we are usually our worst enemy regarding our own creativity but, even if we know we have the idea of the century, selling it to management (or anybody!) can be extremely difficult. The status quo is comfortable, creative change isn't.

Here are some of the things you will hear as you try and sell your new idea:

- It's a great idea but, unfortunately, we don't have the budget
- I like it, but the Legal Department would never agree
- That's all very well in theory, but in my experience...
- You need to be more specific about your proposal
- If it's that good, why hasn't somebody thought of it before?
- Let's wait until the new organisation has settled down
- The savings wouldn't come to this division anyway...
- This is a short-term solution; we're more interested in the long-term
- The intangible risks would be too great

Printed with acknowledgement to the original in IBM South Africa News.

SELLING CREATIVE IDEAS

FORCE FIELD ANALYSIS

DOING YOUR HOMEWORK

Before presenting your new idea to the decision-makers, sit down and do your homework. One way to prepare to take on the 'enemy' (status quo inertia) is to do an analysis of the forces which will be fighting against your idea as well as those which will be pushing in your favour. Example:

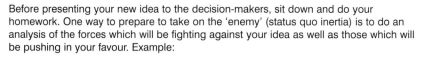

FORCES AGAINST

- No budget
- Boss likes to 'play it safe'
- Shortage of staff
- New technology needed to produce it

FORCES IN FAVOUR

- Creativity is part of our mission
- Customer complaints show need
- Sales in this area are declining
- Competition is innovating
- Boss needs 'brownie points'

You should obviously be specific and mention names and situations. If the left side starts to push the right side off the page then at least you know what you're up against!

FORCE FIELD ANALYSIS

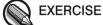 EXERCISE

To get some practice with Force Field Analysis, think of an idea you'd like to have implemented in your organisation and note down some of the opposing forces:

FORCES AGAINST	FORCES IN FAVOUR

SELLING CREATIVE IDEAS

CHIPS ANALYSIS

OVERCOMING THE BARRIERS

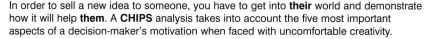

In order to sell a new idea to someone, you have to get into **their** world and demonstrate how it will help **them**. A **CHIPS** analysis takes into account the five most important aspects of a decision-maker's motivation when faced with uncomfortable creativity.

C osts
- Give an estimate of how much the idea will cost to implement.
- Show how much it will save.
- Point out long-term ROI benefits.

H elp
- All managers like (and are paid) to help if they can. Appeal to the coaching, development and leadership role of the decision-maker.

I nnovation
- Stress the positive side of newness. Decision-makers are responsible for innovating - it's on their job description!

P restige
- Highlight what's in it for them.
- Work on how you can make the decision-maker look good and gain prestige within the organisation.

S ecurity
- Above all, show why the idea is a 'safe bet'. Stress reliability, quality and low risk aspects. If it **is** risky, outline 'Plan B'.

CHIPS ANALYSIS

 EXERCISE

Using the example you chose for your force field exercise, now imagine that you're going to present the idea to your boss or another decision-maker. Jot down some of the arguments you might use:

C osts _____

H elp _____

I nnovation _____

P restige _____

S ecurity _____

SELLING CREATIVE IDEAS

PRESENTATION TIPS

STRUCTURE

B ang!
- Always start with an attention-getting 'hook'

O pening
- Outline main messages (Road Map)

M essage
- Give only 4-5 key messages

B ridge
- Make a bridge between each key message and your **CHIPS** analysis of the decision-maker's needs

E xamples
- Give frequent examples to help the audience visualise what you mean

R ecap
- Be sure to summarise and conclude

B ang!
- Always finish with a closing 'hook'

Bomber B is a mnemonic device to help you structure your presentation and make it fly!

PRESENTATION TIPS

V.H.F. SUPPORT

A creative idea deserves a creative presentation. Here are some tips:

Visual aids
- Show pictures, graphs and diagrams - few words
- Use colour • Introduce humour
- Change medium frequently (overhead projector, flipchart, 35 mm projector, whiteboard, etc)

Hearing support
- Use tape player for 'atmosphere' music or sound effects
- Slow down and articulate well

Feeling support
- Give frequent examples and anecdotes from **their** world
- Use parables and analogies • Evoke emotions of pride, belongingness, teamwork, etc • Appeal to sense of touch, taste and smell whenever possible

PRESENTATION TIPS

PLATFORM SKILLS

When, at last, you're on your feet in front of the decision-makers, concentrate on **You** and **Them**:

YOU
- Keep your body language 'open' • Be a lighthouse with eye contact
- Head up, voice up! • If possible, move around • Exaggerate gestures
- Beware of coins in pocket/playing with markers

THEM
- Welcome interruptions • **Reflect** questions back to the poser to make sure you've understood ("If I understand correctly you'd be interested in ...") and then **deflect** it for group comment before giving your opinion • Ask questions yourself as often as possible to get objections out in the open
- Play devil's advocate to pre-empt argument ("What are some of the reasons you feel this **won't** work?") • Don't show impatience or anger with objections - it will make it easier for them to kill your idea

TOTAL 100%

SELLING CREATIVE IDEAS

CREATIVITY & MANAGEMENT

'IT'S NOT CREATIVE UNLESS IT SELLS'

REFERENCE & FURTHER READING

'The Act of Creation', Arthur Koestler, Penguin 1989

'The Use of Lateral Thinking', Edward de Bono, Penguin 1990

'In Search of Excellence', Peters and Waterman, Harper Collins 1995

'Innovation and Entrepreneurship', Peter Drucker, Heinemann 1985

'Moments of Truth', Jan Carlzon, Harper and Row 1991

'The Dinosaur Strain', Mark Brown, The Innovation Centre 1993

'Use Your Head', Tony Buzan, BBC Publications 1995

'The Brain Book', Peter Russell, Routledge and Kegan Paul 1990

'Archie and the Eureka Workshops', John Townsend, Industrial and Commercial Training (Journal) May/June 1986

'L'Instant Creatif', Florence Vidal, Editions Flammarion 1984

'L'Innovation en Matiere de Produits', B.P.S. Berne 1977

- Answer to 'Puzzles': 5 + 5 + 5 = 550; √1 = 1
- Answer to 'Who Does What?': Manager: Jane Simpson, Lawyer: Ted Anderson, Accountant: Fred Harris, Secretary: Sam Carter, Clerk: Peter Thomas

About the Authors

John Townsend, BA MA MIPD is Managing Director of the Master Trainer Institute. He founded the Institute after 30 years of experience in international consulting and human resource management positions in the UK, France, the United States and Switzerland.

From 1978-1984 he was European Director of Executive Development with GTE in Geneva with training responsibility for over 800 managers in some 15 countries. Mr Townsend has published a number of management and professional guides and regularly contributes articles to leading management and training journals. In addition to training trainers, he is also a regular speaker at conferences and leadership seminars throughout Europe.

The late **Jacques-Patrick Favier** graduated from Grenoble University with a degree in political science before embarking on a career in human resource management. After more than 20 years' experience in the multinational and public administration arena in France and Switzerland, he set up his own company 'Eureka Training' based at the foot of the Jura mountains. He specialised in creativity seminars and also undertook management and interpersonal skills workshops for well-known Swiss banks, insurance companies and pharmaceutical giants. He also taught operational creativity to managers at the Geneva Industrial Institute.

Published by **Management Pocketbooks Ltd**
Laurel House, Station Approach, Alresford, Hants SO24 9JH, U.K. Tel: +44 (0)1962 735573
Fax: +44 (0)1962 733637   E-mail: sales@pocketbook.co.uk   Website: www.pocketbook.co.uk

Editions: 1st 1991 (ISBN 1 870471 07 5),
          2nd 1998 (ISBN 1 870471 69 5)
Reprinted 1999, 2001, 2003   Printed in UK

British Library Cataloguing-in-Publication Data –
A catalogue record for this book is available
from the British Library.

ORDER FORM

Your details

Name _____

Position _____

Company _____

Address _____

_____

_____

Telephone _____

Facsimile _____

E-mail _____

VAT No. (EC companies) _____

Your Order Ref _____

Please send me:

No. copies

The _Creative Manager's_ _____ Pocketbook [ ]

The _____ Pocketbook [ ]

The _____ Pocketbook [ ]

The _____ Pocketbook [ ]

The _____ Pocketbook [ ]

Order by Post

MANAGEMENT POCKETBOOKS LTD
LAUREL HOUSE, STATION APPROACH, ALRESFORD,
HAMPSHIRE SO24 9JH UK

Order by Phone, Fax or Internet

Telephone: +44 (0)1962 735573
Facsimile: +44 (0)1962 733637
E-mail: sales@pocketbook.co.uk
Web: www.pocketbook.co.uk

Customers in USA should contact:
Stylus Publishing, LLC, 22883 Quicksilver Drive,
Sterling, VA 20166-2012
Telephone: 703 661 1581 or 800 232 0223
Facsimile: 703 661 1501 E-mail: styluspub@aol.com